INCAR?

Affirmations:

(EXPECTATION)

Small furry animals are aln̲ ... .∪∪ ∪∪ ∪u.∪∪ an "ooh!" of delight from small children, in much the same way as human babies seem designed to elicit "cooing" sounds from maternal women. Their apparent innocence, and helplessness, seems to bring out the best in so many people. Another by-product of these emotions is to encourage us to try to keep things as they are. How often has it been said, for example, "what a pity that they have to grow-up!"

For so many people Christmas is tied-up with all of these emotions and unspoken yearnings, writ large. It is all too often an excuse for a binge of nostalgia. Children have become the subjects of Christmas, and Christ the victim. Christ Himself is stripped of his manhood and has become little more than the universal baby, innocent, helpless, and unthreatening. He has been hedged about and enclosed in a womb from which there is no escape.

If the story of Christmas came to be written today it could well be the start of a heroic rags-to-riches saga. In fact Christmas is the beginning of a cave to cave story, for a womb is a kind of cave, and a cave became a kind of womb.

It is all too easy in our modern world to see the baby and overlook the God, yet both were there. The Almighty God who created the heavens and all they contain, the galaxies and the stars; who created the world and all it holds; who created the smallest atomic particle; who created the angels and archangels, and who created humanity, entered and allowed Himself to be constrained within a young woman's womb. That same God, the Son of the Almighty Father, was born in a cave, which doubled as a stable, and the representatives of creation came together to witness and wonder.

1

The angels, the animals, the people, the star, all bore witness.

"Oh Figaro, look, look, the wishing star!
Star-light, star-bright, the first star I see tonight.
I wish I may, I wish I might, have the wish I make tonight!"

These famous words are spoken by the puppet-maker Giupetto, at the beginning of Walt Disney's classic Pinocchio. Giupetto wished for a real boy, and his wish came true, but he would not have been the first or the last to make a wish; to wish upon a star.

Two thousand years ago the royal wise men, or Magi, did much the same thing. They were probably 'wise' in the ways of astrology, rather than astronomy, and felt able to interpret the sign of a new star in the heavens. Perhaps the star was a sign from God, indicating the birth of His Son as a man, or perhaps the voice of God was to be found in the unspoken wishes of the Magi, projected onto otherwise indifferent celestial phenomena. Perhaps the truth lies somewhere in between these two poles. Either way, the question remains as to what they wished for as they gazed up into the sky on that fateful night.

It is likely that the Magi wished for peace and prosperity, for themselves and for other people. They took with them gold as a gift for the Child, gold which is a symbol of worldly wealth, power and kingship. They hoped to find a King who would rule in wisdom and justice, and in this they represented the aspirations of all men. As with Giupetto, their wish was granted.

They also yearned to find God. Their souls must have thirsted for God, the living God, even as their bodies thirsted for water through the parched lands of the Arabian desert, and so they brought incense with which to worship. Their search for God was fuelled by the wish to fill the emptiness of their heathen souls. As with so many people today they longed to find a meaning in life, perhaps longed to find Life itself. As with Giupetto, their wish was granted.

The third gift brought by the Magi was Myrrh, and as with the other two it expressed their inmost desires. They sought a king, and they sought God, and finally they sought the bridge-builder between the two kingdoms, a High Priest. What they found was the Priest King, of the order of Melchizedek, and they brought the myrrh oil with which to anoint him, and proclaim Him. As with Giupetto, their wish was granted. The full significance of their action, though, could not have been clear to them, for their choice of myrrh was also prophetic. The myrrh they brought foreshadowed not only the priest, but the victim, for it pointed towards Christ's death and burial. Myrrh mixed with wine was given to Our Lord on the cross, it was also used to embalm His lifeless corpse for the tomb.

The Magi followed a star, and found a Star, Christ who is the Morning Star which never sets. When we gaze upon that Morning Star and wish-pray, the desires of our hearts are revealed. They are revealed for all to see, although we ourselves are all too often the last to see. They are discovered by the way we put our prayer into action. Perhaps our secret prayer, not the one we would admit to, is for worldly wealth, power, and kingship...for ourselves. Perhaps it is for glory...for ourselves. Or perhaps, like the Magi, we come in humility, searching for God, for His sake. If so, we like the Magi shall surely find the object of our desires.

(REALISATION)

St. John tells us that "the Word became flesh and dwelt among us." These words are at the heart of the Christian faith. They describe the new relationship between God and Man. The relationship created in Christ, which is

3

summed-up in the word *Incarnation*.

It is impossible for us to 'picture' God, the God who made everything from the smallest atom to the largest galaxy; He is so great that our imaginings can never 'do Him justice'. That is why, in the first of the Ten Commandments, we were forbidden to "make any graven image" of Him, in case we were tempted to cut God down to our own size! On the other hand we are told that we are made in His image, yet however much we try, we can never live up to that description of ourselves.

In spite of these problems, impossible for us to overcome, God wants us to know and love Him. Since we cannot find Him, however hard we try, God has revealed Himself to us, over and over again! In the Old Testament we can read the story of God's attempts to show Himself to the world through the prophets, and through His dealings with the Jewish people. In all of this God was preparing for the time when He would not only show us what He is *like*, but show us *Himself*!

Most people, at one time or another, have felt *sympathy* for another person. Sometimes this feeling is impersonal, and for people whom we have never known. Sometimes we feel for people who are very close to us. Sympathy enables us to get alongside the other person/people by imagining what they might be experiencing, but it does not enable us to truly share their suffering. Neither does sympathy give the other person confidence that we can do anything about their problem! What is required is *empathy*, not merely imagination, not merely walking alongside, but personal experience which enables us to step into their shoes.

God has shown us Himself by stepping into our shoes. He did this by enabling a man to live-up to the description 'made in the image of God'. Jesus could only

4

be the 'perfect' Man, though, if He was also the *pattern* on which Man was modelled: *God Himself.*

The world is rather like an artist's painting, the artist being God. To the tutored eye the subtle differences of brush-technique, use of colour, style and the like is often enough to reveal the identity of the artist. To most of us, though, and even to the expert, the most important indication is the signature of the artist. The signature of God is all the goodness and beauty we see around us. Of all of God's creations, however, His masterpiece is Mankind. We are no mere landscape or still-life, "God created Man in His own image''; we are God's self-portrait! There is no need of subtle techniques to identify the artist, nor even of a signature. What is needed is some acquaintance with the artist Himself!

The problem lies in what has been done to the painting. All too often the image has been so scored, creased, and generally defaced, that the original portrait has become all-but unrecognisable. The reality of God the Father can then only be clearly perceived in the works and Person of God the Son, for God the Son is the extension of God the Father into our knowable world. Thus a bridge is established between the unknowable and 'immutable', or changeless and self-sufficient God, and the world which is His creation.

A helpful metaphor might be that of a hologram, or three dimensional image, where the two dimensional original is hidden from view. It is only by extending itself into three dimensions that the two-dimensional original can be apprehended. This does not mean that God the Father in Himself lacks anything, nor that the Father and the Son are indistinguishable, rather, that the Father cannot possibly be seen apart from the Son.

It is only in the person of Christ that we see God's BEING expressed clearly. Without the Son or 'Word'

5

there would be no link between the unknowable God and the world. In fact without the Son there would be no world, for the world does not co-exist with God. It is totally dependent upon God's continuing creative activity. God's creativity, in turn, is dependent upon His 'ability' to effect change without Himself being changed. Without the 'Word' the BEING of God would have no means of doing anything whilst remaining unmoved and changeless. In sharing a human life and death, and rising from the grave, God has shown us Himself without being compromised. He has also repaired the relationship between Mankind and Himself and, what is more, He has opened a door for us which would have been unthinkable before. In the *Incarnation* of Christ, God and Man were united, never again to be separated and Man has been perfected in God's image.

(CONTINUITY)

Many Christians tend to think of the Incarnation solely in terms of the earthly ministry of Christ, but in doing so they are seriously mistaken. St. Paul describes the Church as the Body of Christ, with Christ Himself as the head. As a metaphor this expresses the Truth that the Incarnation has not come to an end, but rather has been perpetuated and extended in the Church, corporately and in the lives of individual Christians, by virtue of their incorporation into the Church. In taking His inclusive Manhood with Him when He ascended, He permits us to share in the eternal life of God!

The first man in outer space was the Russian cosmonaut Yuri Gagarin. In those days Russia was ruled by Marxist communists, who believe that there is no God. Although Yuri Gagarin's space flight was a great human achievement, it was marred by being used for propaganda purposes. One of the first things which Gagarin said was along the lines of: ''Well, I'm up here and I can't see God anywhere!''

6

It is not only communists who think like that; a great many Christians, including some theologians, think along the same lines. They believe that since God is clearly not "up there" in the sky, Christ cannot have ascended into heaven, and so the story must be untrue or misleading. The truth is that Christ not only *did* ascend, but *had* to ascend to His Father in heaven. This does not mean, however, that 'heaven' is a place somewhere in the sky.

Arguably one of the most enduring images on film is that of the Western hero, having done his good deeds, riding off into the distance. This kind of ending leaves the viewer 'hanging', hoping for more. The image encourages the imagination to believe that the hero has not actually left, but has merely moved to another part of our world. One is almost tempted to believe that if one went off in search of him, sooner or later one would find him. On the other hand the image of somebody *rising* into the air and disappearing is the most powerful symbol of leaving this world altogether.

The sense of finality is etched into the consciousness of the witnesses in a way that no other leave-taking could have achieved. It emphasised the futility of searching for "the living amongst the dead" (Luke ch24 v5)! The Ascension, though, was no mere symbol. It happened, for only by returning to His Father, taking His Manhood with Him and thus continuing the Incarnation, could He keep open the door to heaven.

The means whereby the Incarnation is extended into the Church is through the Sacraments. In the Sacrament of the Eucharist the extension of the Incarnation into the Church is seen most clearly. God takes the ordinary things of this world, in this case bread and wine, and makes of them the extraordinary means of His real presence, objectively, amongst us.

7

Christ promised that the bread would become His flesh, and the wine His blood, and as with all living people His presence is inseparable from the presence of His living body. The miracle of the Incarnation is brought into the midst of the Church each time the priest utters the words of Christ with the intention that Christ's promise be fulfilled.

It is worthy of note that when Christ said those words, and spoke of recalling Himself into our present, He had not yet died, and it must therefore be the Incarnate Christ which is recalled for His promise to be kept and intelligible! Since there is only one Christ, who makes Himself present amongst us in and through the Eucharistic elements, the Risen and Ascended Christ must also be the Incarnate Christ.

The Book of Common Prayer defines sacraments as ''effectual signs of grace'', in which the same way as a smile is an outward and visible sign of happiness. A smile not only reflects one's mood, but contributes to creating that mood, in the person concerned, and in those around him. Sacraments work in a similar way. The Sacraments of the Church both demonstrate symbolically what God does through them, and are the very means whereby God achieves the demonstrated effect.

A useful image is that of a reservoir high-up in the hills. Such a reservoir is like God, in that without its water the crops in the valley fields would fail and there could be no life. The problem is in getting the water from the reservoir to the valley. This is achieved by providing, in this case, seven channels or canals from the reservoir to the valley; the seven Sacraments. By means of these seven Sacraments Christ provides for all the possible needs of the Church, and through them guarantees the present active power of the Holy Spirit. This is not to say that God confines Himself to the Sacraments, but that only in the Sacraments does He *guarantee* His presence. In and through the Sacraments Christ is united with His Church, and thus with the World, with an intimacy only to be found elsewhere in the union of a Bride and Groom.

In the Gospel according to St. John, Our Lord tells Nicodemus that in order for a man to enter the Kingdom of Heaven it is necessary for him to be born again of water and the spirit. This is exactly what happens when a person is baptised. Just as the two sides of Christ's nature, or rather His two natures, cannot be separated, neither can the two components of Baptism be separated. A person cannot be 'baptised in the Spirit', without the accompanying rite of baptism in water, any more than could the Son of God also have become the Son of Man without first entering into the Virgin's womb and taking flesh of her flesh.

At every baptism, whether child or adult, the miracle of the Incarnation is once again witnessed. It is not without reason that Eastern Orthodox Christians talk of the Deification of men: the re-making of men into God, by adoption! The Eucharist and Baptism are only two of the seven sacraments of the Church, albeit the two most important, but in and through them all the Incarnation is expressed and extended. They are the channels through which He delivers, or imparts, the effects of His life, death and resurrection; and the power which enables the Sacraments. The Holy Spirit, as He was the Power which brought about the conception of the Lord and His Incarnation.